1 MONTH OF
FREE
READING

at

www.ForgottenBooks.com

By purchasing this book you are eligible for one month membership to ForgottenBooks.com, giving you unlimited access to our entire collection of over 1,000,000 titles via our web site and mobile apps.

To claim your free month visit:

www.forgottenbooks.com/free1120901

ISBN 978-0-331-41668-8
PIBN 11120901

Forgotten Books is a registered trademark of FB &c Ltd.
Copyright © 2018 FB &c Ltd.
FB &c Ltd, Dalton House, 60 Windsor Avenue, London, SW19 2RR.
Company number 08720141. Registered in England and Wales.

For support please visit www.forgottenbooks.com

Historic, archived document

Do not assume content reflects current
scientific knowledge, policies, or practices.

WEEKLY STATION REPORTS

OF THE OFFICE OF

DRY LAND AGRICULTURE INVESTIGATIONS

BUREAU OF PLANT INDUSTRY

U. S. DEPARTMENT OF AGRICULTURE

REPORTS FOR THE WEEK ENDING APRIL 11, 1931.

JUDITH BASIN:

      The past winter has been one of the mildest as well as one
of the driest winters that have occurred since the station was started.
Only during one month, October, of the fall and winter have the amount
of precipitation or the mean temperature approached the average. The
amount of moisture during October, 1.99 inches, is more than the total
amount that has fallen since November 1. Since that time only 1.47 inches
has been recorded and only .18 inch or this has fallen during April. The
only other winters during which a smaller amount of precipitation fell at
the station were 1920-21 with 1.29 inches from November 1 to April 1 and
1925-26 when 1.07 inches fell during the same time.

      The mild, open winter has been very beneficial as far as
wintering livestock is concerned but has been disastrous for winter
wheat. Soil blowing has been very prevalent since January and is
gradually increasing in severity. Soil drifting occurred 14 days during
March. Some fields have blown worse than others, particularly those
fields on which all of the summer fallow operations were done with a
one-way disk. Following several weeks of high temperatures the
thermometer dropped to 5 degrees below and 4 degrees below on March 25
and March 26, respectively. Winter wheat that had started to green up
was killed back to the surface of the ground and that which had suffered
the greastest damage from soil blowing and drifting was killed entirely.
Although it is too early to tell definitely, the killing of winter wheat
in this section will be considerable. On the rotation plots only those
plots seeded on green manure fallow are showing much signs of life. In
the Cereal project most of the date of seeding plots have survived while
in the variety test only some of the new winter hardy hybrids are alive.
A commercial field of 35 acres of Karmont seeded on fallow on the station
looks very good.

      Spring plowing on the rotations was started April 8 and
completed April 10. There is sufficient moisture in the soil to make
conditions almost ideal for plowing. Other work this week has consisted
in getting ground ready for planting trees.
      Maximum temperature 72; minimum 25; precipitation, none.

HAVRE:

The past winter has been unusually mild. There was a storm of rather short duration in November but the following three months were all much above the normal. Precipitation has been about normal except for February, when there was only a trace.

Field work was started the last week in March and has been interrupted by two snow storms.

Winter wheat apparently has survived the winter in very good shape. The snow storm on April 1, when a minimum temperature of nine (9) degrees was recorded, seems to have caused some injury. However, stands seem to be very good on all methods.

Native grasses are making a small amount of growth. Brome-grass and crested wheat grass are green. There apparently has been more than the usual amount of killing in slender wheat grass. Alfalfa seems to have survived the winter in pretty fair shape.

Stored moisture is rather low in fallow. Stubble land is moist to between 8 and 12 inches in depth. While soil moisture samplings have not been taken yet this spring, samplings last fall showed that summer fallow was much below the normal and there has been very little accumulation during the winter months.

Some of the early dates of seeding have been made. Weeds have made a fair start. Present indications are that our main seeding can be cone a little sooner than usual.

There have been a few very windy days during the last 10 days. Russian thistles have blown a great deal and have caused considerable damage to fences. While the soil in this particular section has not blown extensively, there are sections where some damage has been done from drifting.

Maximum temperature 75; minimum 30; precipitation, .51 inch.

November to April 11			
	Maximum	Minimum	Precipitation
November	66	-14	.50
December	47	3	.22
January	54	- 6	.48
February	56	15	Trace
March	60	- 3	.47
April, to 11th.	75	30	.51

HUNTLEY:

The past winter was one of the mildest and driest in the history of this section of Montana. Minimum temperatures of zero or below have to date been recorded on but five days since October 1. The lowest temperature reached during the winter was 12 below zero. Maximum daily temperatures of 60 or above were not infrequent. High winds were recorded on a few days and as is often the case during such an open winter some soil drifting took place doing more or less damage to winter wheat on exposed locations. Snow-fall was heavy in October but scanty during the succeeding months and seldom remained on the ground for more than two or three days at a time.

Some field work was carried on by farmers during parts of January, February, and March. At the station the only "out of season" tillage consisted of harrowing down cloddy fall-plowed land on both the irrigated and dry-land fields.

Thin stands of winter wheat and rye survived the season which was rather unfavorable for such crops. A good growth was made during the latter part of March but an abrupt drop in temperature to zero or a few degrees above for three or four days killed back much of the wheat. The crop is recovering slowly and the fields are again beginning to look quite green.

Plowing and tillage for small grains has been completed and the seed beds obtained were much finer than those of a year ago. Spring wheat and peas have been sown and oats and barley are being planted to-day.
Maximum temperature 80; minimum 25; precipitation, none.

SHERIDAN:

The past winter was extremely mild and dry. Temperatures were below zero only four times during the winter, 1 below in November 8 below in January, and 2 below twice the last week in March. Precipitation was sufficient only to moisten the surface for a short period a few times during the winter, the surface being dry most of the time until late in March. Some field work was accomplished in this section every month of the winter, and some seeding of winter wheat was done near the station the last week in December.

- 4 -

Sheridan, continued:

Fall rains were sufficient to moisten the ground to a depth of from 5 to 6 inches. All fall seeded grain came through the winter in good condition. Wheat seeded the middle of October emerged some time during the winter after the first of January and before the middle of March. The seeding of November 1 emerged about the middle of March.

Summer fallow and fall plowing in Field G was cultivated with the duckfoot cultivator, the remainder of Field G was plowed, and a few of the rotation plots plowed the week ending March 21. At that time the plow rode on dry soil at a depth of from four to five inches, but the surface to that depth plowed in nice shape. Rain and snow March 22 stopped field work on cultivated land, but about seven acres of sod in Field I was plowed at intervals between storms during the period from March 23 to April 6.

Field work was resumed April 6 and continued throughout the week. Preparation of Field G for seeding was completed and that field, 16 acres, was seeded, 1 acre each to Victory oats and Nepal barley for seed blocks and the remainder to Trebi barley. Preparation of the land and seeding of barley and peas in all of the annual crops pastures was completed. Preparation of the Rotation field for seeding is being completed to-day, April 11, and the check plots of the rotations are being seeded. Extra tillage plots of spring wheat, outside the rotation field, were seeded yesterday. The first date of seeding spring wheat, oats, and barley, was seeded April 6. Fallow for cereal varieties also was duckfooted during the week.

Soil samples taken at random this morning showed moisture to a depth of about 20 inches on small grain stubble, and 12 to 14 inches on fall plowing where small grain was grown last year.

Lambing was in progress throughout the week, with only a small percentage of twins, and one set of triplets.

DICKINSON:

The winter of 1930-31 was one of the mildest of record at Dickinson. Each of the winter months except March was much warmer than normal. Much quiet, calm weather prevailed. Snowfall was light and the ground bare a part of the time. Precipitation was below normal in November, December, and January and a little above average in February and March.

Dickinson, continued:

Frost was out of the soil and the grass was greening up to some extent on March 25, when a mild blizzard sent the temperature down to 9 below zero.

Tillage on the Rotations was started on April 7. Field peas were seeded on April 10 on the three green manure plots. Wheat was seeded on April 11, three days later than in 1930, but near the average date for the seeding of wheat on these plots. The plots are staked ready for seeding oats and barley.

A severe wind on April 8 made field work impossible for a part of the day and caused soil drifting on bare ground, including fallow, potato and corn ground.

Visitors during the week included Director P. F. Trowbridge, and Mr. M. B. Johnson, Agent in Animal Husbandry, Bureau of Animal Industry, U. S. Department of Agriculture.
Maximum temperature 78; minimum 22; precipitation, trace.

MANDAN:

Agronomy

The past winter was the mildest on record in this area and for the State in general. The mean temperature for Bismarck, according to the U. S. Weather Bureau, was 23 degrees F., for December; 25 degrees F., for January; and 30 degrees F., for February, while the usual for the same months is 15, 8 and 10, respectively. The snowfall for the period from November to March was 30 inches according to the Bismarck records. The precipitation for the year to March 31 at the Mandan Station was 2.11 inches, comparing with a 15-year average of 1.27 inches and a 55-year average (for this area) of 1.83 inches. Nearly an inch of rain fell on March 22. The coldest temperature during the winter was 11 degrees below on January 13. The temperature was below zero three times in November, once in December, three times in January, once in February, and three times im March. The mean temperature for March was near normal. A cold spell with snow and high wind, occurred near the end of March.

Field work started on April 6. Spring plowing has been completed and other preparations are nearly complete. Plots should be ready for seeding early next week. The soil is in excellent condition for cultivation, and moisture conditions are favorable for starting small grains, and more favorable than for several years past.

Mandan, continued:

Agronomy, continued.

Crested wheat grass started growth about March 20, but was retarded by the cold weather later. Brome-grass started growth about April 1.

Winter wheat appears to have come through the winter in excellent condition, and a stand remains on fallow for the first time in the history of the station.

A few acres of wheat were seeded in the county near the 25th of March, but most field work did not start until the present week. Some low places are still too wet for cultivation.
Maximum temperature 76; minimum 29; precipitation, none.

Arboriculture

Nursery fields have been disked, dragged and packed. Seed of Caragana, boxelder, green ash, Russian olive, and chokecherry, has been planted.

The hauling in of trees from the heeling-in bed to the packing room is in progress. Russian olive and caragana seedlings are in places badly frozen in, but it is not expected that this will delay the work of shipping which should begin at once.

Horticulture

It appears that most fruit trees and small fruits passed through the winter in good condition, except where damaged by drought and red spiders last summer. Several Compass and Mammoth trees in the spacing experiment are dead, but red spiders are thought to be responsible.

Field work started on April 6, later than has been the case for a number of years. The week has been spent in pruning trees and in preparation of the ground for nursery and strawberry planting.

A fair to good set of most fruits was obtained in the greenhouse from hand crossing work. Apples, plums, cherries, and gooseberries are the kinds of fruits used in this work.

BELLE FOURCHE:

The past winter was the mildest in the history of the station. The temperature did not fall below 9 degrees below, and there were only eight days in which sub-zero temperatures occurred. The severest weather of the season was experienced March 25 and 26 when the temperature dropped to 4 below and 3 below, respectively, and the lowest daily maximum temperatures for the winter were recorded. There were very few high winds, and practically no soil blowing took place. The precipitation was almost negligible, but sufficient moisture was provided by the fall rains to permit all crops to withstand the winter in good condition.

Moderate rains in March were of great benefit to fall grains which survived with perfect stands. Winter wheat, winter rye, and hay and pasture crops resumed spring growth about March 20, but the sub-zero weather which followed did considerable damage to fall grain on the higher and more exposed spots. The injured grain, however, is making a slow recovery.

The spring opened unusually early, and some spring wheat was reported seeded in January. Plowing of rotation plots was commenced March 18, but weather conditions during the remainder of the month were not favorable to field work, and seeding was delayed until the middle of the current week. All dry land rotation plots of spring wheat, oats, barley, field peas, sweet clover, and brome-grass have been seeded.

Sufficient moisture is present in the soil to insure the germination of small grain, but good stands of sweet clover and brome-grass probably will not be obtained until after a beneficial rain is received. As there is no moisture in the soil below the surface for six inches, crop prospects are not particularly encouraging. On summer fallowed land moisture is present to a depth of only 20 inches.

With the exception of a few cool, cloudy days, the present week has been comparatively warm and favorable to crop growth. The highest temperature for the season to date occurred April 7, and the nights have been warmer than heretofore. Strong winds have caused the surface soil to dry rapidly, and additional moisture will soon be needed.
Maximum temperature 80; minimum 29; precipitation, none.

ARDMORE:

The winter of 1930-31 was one of the mildest on record. No below zero temperature was recorded until January 12, when the temperature fell to five degrees below zero. Only one other below zero temperature occurred during the months of January and February. The fields were free from snow during the first part of February and many farmers seeded wheat extensively during that period. Light snows occurred during the latter half of February and the first part of March. The snow disappeared before the middle of March, leaving the fields in excellent condition for planting.

All of the large fields on the station were seeded during the week of March 16.

The plowing and disking on the rotations was completed on March 25. On March 26 the most severe storm of the winter commenced. Only about five inches of snow fell, but this snow was accompanied by high winds and severe cold. On March 27 the temperature fell to 13 degrees below zero, the minimum for the winter. Stock losses due to the storm were very low in this vicinity. Farther south, where rain preceded the snow and where the snowfall was greater, losses were heavy.

It was not possible to resume field work after the storm until April 6. On April 6 and 7 the harrowing for small grains was completed. The condition of the surface soil after harrowing was excellent even on the spring plowed plots. On April 8 the wind velocity was so high that seeding was not attempted. All of the wheat, oats, barley, peas, sweet clover, alfalfa and brome in the rotations were seeded the latter part of the week.

Winter grains came through the winter in good condition, though a few plots were injured by mice and rabbits. Some damage due to soil blowing has been experienced, but all plots appear to have at least a normal stand.

Soil moisture conditions are better than they have been any year since 1927. There is enough moisture present in the soil to give all grain and hay crops a good early start. Precipitation since January 1 is as follows:

January, .02 inch.   February, .36 inch.   March, .73 inch.
April to date, .04 inch.
Maximum temperature 79; minimum 23; precipitation, trace.

AKRON:

The fall of 1930 was favorable for completing all current field experiments. The first snow was in the nature of a blizzard on November 18, which proved severe on livestock. This first snow was heavy and a goodly covering was left over most of the fields as well as deep drifts on the leeward side of obstructions. Many of these deep drifts remained all winter. Another severe blizzard occurred March 27, accompanied with extremely high wind and low temperatures. Suffering among livestock was very severe. With the exception of these two storms the winter season has been open and mild. The lowest minimum temperature yet experienced was five degrees below zero during the recent blizzard.

The fall of 1930 was a little too dry for well established stands of winter wheat on all types of soil preparation. However, winter wheat here on the station and throughout the adjoining countryside seems to have come through the winter satisfactorily. Some soil blowing occurred on two days preceding the blizzard of March 27, on adjoining farms.

Spring opened rather early and cultural and seeding activities were started promptly. The early spring seeded cereal small grain experiments were seeded and the rotation cultural methods plots made ready for seeding before the storm of March 27. Up to the present week it was impossible to resume field work because of wet soil.

The recent storm was very severe to livestock here on the station particularly to the experimental pig and lamb fattening lots and to newly dropped lambs among the ewe flock.

Seeding activities have been stressed all week with the result that practically all early spring seeded small grain experiments are in the ground by this week end.

Mr. H. B. Osland and Mr. Henderson have been here all this past week aiding with the final weights of the pigs and lambs. Dr. D. W. Robertson, Mr. Wayne Austin, and a student helper visited the station Wednesday in the interest of Cereal experiments.

Maximum temperature 76; minimum 23; precipitation, none.

ARCHER:

The winter was mild and dry. The precipitation for
December was, .01 inch; for January, .02 inch; for February, .27 inch,
for March, .25 inch; and for April, to date, .02 inch. The coldest
temperature, eight degrees below, was recorded March 27. The next
coldest temperature, two degrees, was recorded January 9. December
was rather windy but since then until the latter part of March there
was no soil blowing. During the latter part of March and the first
part of April severe soil blowing occurred.

Winter wheat came through the windy period without serious
damage. That seeded with the common drill has maintained a full stand.

The wind and dry weather severely injured some of the evergreens. This is especially true of the Jack pine. Some of the Black
Hills spruce have had their leaves cut away by soil blowing.

The dairy cattle did well during the winter. Only during
short periods was it necessary to keep them in the barn at night. This
condition was favorable for a good milk flow and the maintaining of good
flesh.

Field work started April 6. Since then all of the spring
plowing, harrowing, and most of the duckfooting of the rotation plots
have been accomplished. The preparation of soil and the seeding of
the varieties of spring wheats, barleys, and oats were finished
April 8. The dates of seeding were started March 15 and have been
followed up since that date. About 95 acres in the dairy field have
been tilled with the one-way disk and the trees on the north of the
farmstead are being cultivated to-day.
Maximum temperature 67; minimum 18; precipitation, none.

NORTH PLATTE:

The mild winter was continued into March. First field work
on the station was done on March 2. Preparation of ground for seeding
spring grains progressed with several interruptions and spring wheat
plots were seeded on March 16. Other interruptions followed, culminating
in a blizzard of unusual severity on March 26 and 27. Temperatures
dropped to zero, traffic was suspended, and the losses of livestock in
many localities ran into high percentages. The snow drifted badly and
field work was not resumed until April 6. Barley, oats, peas, alfalfa
and spring wheat began emerging on April 9. The condition of winter
wheat is excellent. Some freezing occurred during the storm but recovery

North Platte, continued:

is now complete and the growth much in advance of normal for the
season. No winter loss has occurred.

The storage of subsoil moisture is better than for any
season, with possibly one or two exceptions in the history of the
station.

Visitors last week end included Dean Burr of the Agricultural
College and a committee from the Nebraska Senate.

GARDEN CITY:

Spring work started about March 1. Most of the early field work
was done on the new field taken over for dry land investigations in
winter wheat production. Plots had to be trimmed, soil samples taken,
surveys for permanent corner posts made and other work connected with
the new project occupied most of the outside field work during the
month. There are 51 plots devoted to tillage investigations with wheat
in this new work outlined.

Spring plowing started on the dry land project April 9. The
new instrument yard has been set to buffalo sod during the past two weeks.

Small grains were seeded on March 12. This is three weeks
earlier than they have been seeded in the past. All are up and show a
good stand.

Wheat is making exceptional heavy growth for this time of the
year. Much of the wheat on fallows is six to eight inches high and very
thick on the ground.

The ground is well supplied with moisture in the upper three
feet. 1.11 inches of rain fell during January, February, and March,
which is above normal. During April to date .54 inch has fallen.

The minimum temperature during the severe storm two weeks ago
was four degrees above zero. Much of the wheat shows tips frosted but
is coming out of that condition fast.

COLBY:

        This has been a favorable season in most respects so far. January and February were pleasant and unusually warm. There was no precipitation in January and none in February until the last week, when over one and a half inches fell in the form of rain and snow.

        March was unsettled for the most part with almost three times the normal precipitation. During March 26 and 27 this section was in the grip of one of the very worst blizzards ever experienced. About 10 inches of snow fell in the course of about 20 hours. For over 28 hours the wind, blowing a gale from the northwest, and accompanied by temperatures ranging between 10 above and 2 below zero, piled the snow in huge drifts and made it practically impossible for humans or animals to venture out. In this vicinity only one human life was lost but thousands of cattle, sheep and hogs perished. Many farmers lost almost all the livestock they had. All the fruit buds were also killed, but otherwise no injury to crops resulted. The winter wheat, which had survived the winter with practically no killing, was not injured by this cold spell, except that the tips of the leaves which protruded above the snow were frozen back.

        The weather during April thus far has been rather unsettled, comparatively low temperatures alternating with unusually high temperatures. The spring grains which were sown during the third week in March are just beginning to show above ground. Winter wheat, which had been making considerable growth up to the time of the storm, has started growing again and is now from three to eight inches high, the heaviest growth being on fallow and the lightest on corn, sorghum, and bean ground.

        The first soil samples of the season were taken this week. There is an abundance of moisture in all plots to a depth of from nearly four to beyond six feet. There is considerably more moisture in the soil this spring than at any time since 1924.

    Maximum temperature 82; minimum 29; precipitation, none.

    Precipitation from January 1 to March 31, 3.65 inches, normal 1.76 inches
       "   for January, 1931, none, normal .28 inch.
       "   " February,1931, 1.51 inches, normal .60 inch.
       "   " March, 1931, 2.14 inches, normal .84 inch.

HAYS:

Winter wheat has made a very heavy growth except on plots
having little or no tillage. It is extremely heavy on fallow. The
growth on plowing, listing and other methods of similar nature is very
heavy but has lost part of its dark green color, having some yellow
blades at the ground, and growth during the past few days does not
seem so rapid. On ground where wheat was drilled without tillage, such
as stubbled in, or after burning off the stubble, the growth is very
thin and spindling. On fallow and on some of the other plots having
heaviest growth, it is six inches high and beginning to joint.

Barley, oats, and spring wheat, are all up to a good stand,
and uniform on all preparations except on listed ground where it is
streaked, having been a little slower germinating where the lister
furrows had been filled with loose dirt. The weeds are coming very
thick on some of the plots, especially on the listed and spring plowed
plots. On the listed plots it looks like the grain will have a poor
chance to make anything on account of the weeds.

Canada field peas are up to a good stand and looking fine.
Brome-grass is coming through the ground and at present the indications
are fair for a good stand.

Trimming winter wheat plots is the big job on hand at this
time. Staking for this work is well along and the edges marked out on
fields A, B, and C. The wheat is so heavy a stirring plow will have to
be used in many places to destroy the wheat in roads and alleys.

Generally, the weather has been fair. Previous rains
together with the small amount recorded for this week has kept the
ground too wet and sticky for satisfactory field work, except for
staking of plots and general routine work.
Maximum temperature 87; minimum 24; precipitation, .42 inch.

TUCUMCARI:

The first three months of 1931 were very low in wind movement, unusually high in precipitation, and extremely varied in temperature.
This winter and spring there have been less than ten days of seriously
high wind movement, and soil blowing has been less of a problem than
usual. Precipitation for the three months beginning with January has
been exceeded in only two years since records have been kept, 1905 and
1919. Temperatures in January were slightly lower than the long-time

Tucumcari, continued:

mean, February was somewhat warmer than usual, while March was unusually
cold, its mean temperature lower than that of February.

The minimum temperature of the year to date was five degrees
above zero, January 12. February minimum was 24 degrees, while the
coldest in March was 11 above zero, just three days after a maximum of
84 degrees was reached. The extremes for April to date are 82 and 30.

Field work to date consists almost solely of listing. During
the winter a fence was run along one side of the new quarter section,
mesquite and yucca were grubbed from a portion of this land, and a small
area will be cropped this season.

Some 1,200 Chinese elms have been planted along field borders
and in contour rows, while about the same number of evergreen seedlings
were planted in contour rows. Raking and burning of trash and debris
around the station buildings have engaged most of the station force the
past few days.

Fruit prospects are promising in spite of low temperatures at
the close of March. Pears are loaded with blooms, a few peach trees
have a few blossoms, apple buds are showing pink, while Compass cherry-
plums are heavily loaded with blossoms.

Wheat on the plains portion of the county is in excellent
condition and promises the highest acre yield on record. The acreage
is probably greater than ever before.
·Maximum temperature 82; minimum 31; wind velocity, 5.3 miles per hour.

DALHART:

The past winter was characterized by mild temperatures and
an absence of snow. The worst cold spell and snow of the winter season
came the last week of March when a minimum of seven above zero was
recorded for a low of the year. The early fruit trees were blooming
when the cold spell came. Some of the cherries appear to be uninjured
but other tree-fruit is killed.

Dalhart, continued:

Winter wheat and winter rye are growing rapidly and have more than the normal amount of growth for this time of the year. There was no winterkilling and no abandonment of acreage. Prospects are quite similar to the spring of 1929.

Cats and barley were injured by high winds after emergence and again by the low temperatures described above. They present a very poor appearance at the present time.

There is ample moisture in the soil for plants to start growth now. The soil was getting very dry before the moisture came the last of March.

The early flowering shrubs were completely nipped by the low temperatures.

Work for the week has consisted of planting some evergreen varieties and planting of trees and shrubs and cleaning up of winter accumulated trash around the trees. Field work has consisted of the turning under of winter rye in the vineyard and cultivation of trees and trimming a few plots.
Maximum temperature 80; minimum 30; precipitation, none.
Wind velocity, 6.3 miles per hour; evaporation, 1.296 inches.

BIG SPRING:

Weather conditions during the past winter have been rather unusual in many respects. Temperatures throughout the winter were considerably above normal, with only a very few days when the minimum thermometer registered below 20 degrees above zero. Unfortunately two of these times occurred during the latter part of March when the peach, plum, and pear trees were in full bloom or had just dropped their blossoms. As a result of this freeze, nearly all varieties of these fruits will be a failure this year. Many of the shrubs had their new and tender growth frozen back.

Rainfall has been considerably above normal for the first three months of this year. During this time 3.48 inches of rain have been received, while the normal for this same period is 1.99 inches. With the favorable soil moisture conditions prevailing since last fall, most all farmers of this section have been able to get their land prepared in good shape for the coming crop year.

Big Spring, continued:

       With the exception of the M. C. A. plots and the fallows the station spring plowing has been completed.

       An additional 80 acres of land adjoining the station has been leased, and will be used for growing feed crops, which will be used in cattle feeding work.

       The winter wheat plots made a good growth during the winter, but are now showing the effects of the lack of moisture.

       Mr. R. E. Karper, Vice Director of the Texas Experiment Station, Mr. J. M. Jones, Chief of the Animal Husbandry Division of the Texas Station, and Mr. John Simpson, Agricultural Agent for the Texas and Pacific Railroad, were station visitors on April 6.

       Maximum temperature 89; minimum 33; precipitation, .15 inch.

LAWTON:

       One of the mildest winters on record with a minimum temperature of 17 degrees was a boom to this country which possessed so little feed and shelter for humans and livestock. Small grain crops, wheat, oats and barley provided abundant pasturage in most instances for such livestock as was retained by drought stricken farmers.

       A great many agencies of relief, local, state and national have been very active throughout the winter. Seed and feed loans both state and federal have also been extensively used. However, all of the above agencies have found the burden lighter in this county where farm programs are by necessity more diversified than in adjoining counties that have in recent years enjoyed so much temporary prosperity by growing such crops as cotton to the exclusion of practically everything else.

       Optimum moisture conditions favored the growth and development of small grains during the winter. Wheat made only about normal growth, even where unpastured. Although the winter growth of wheat was not as rank as was anticipated the present condition of the crop is the best that has been observed for several years.

       All plantings of winter oats and winter barley made a vigorous winter growth and are well advanced in development.

Lawton, continued:

Fall seedings of alfalfa made as late as the middle of October survived the winter in excellent condition. Some earlier seedings that were made the fore part of September were choked out by a heavy growth of winter grass, and reseeding in the spring was necessary.

In the sweet clover seeding project good stands have been secured on all seeding dates from December 15 to date.

Corn was planted in the rotation plots March 11 in excellent seedbeds, but March temperatures were so cold that only a small percentage of a stand is in sight. The crop will be replanted within a day or two.

The rate and date spring oats project was started January 21, and subsequent seedings up to March 10, the final date, produced good stands. The variety test of spring oats was seeded February 3, and all plots now show satisfactory stands and condition.

Preparations for the approaching new crop season throughout the farm territory in this section were stimulated in January and February by a continuation of abnormally mild weather, and a large acreage of oats was seeded. Wherever the farmer did not have to negotiate a federal loan for seed, the planting was done at an early date. Otherwise the plantings were very appreciably delayed. Range and livestock conditions were reported good in February with the winter-carrying charges reduced to a minimum.

March weather was responsible for some disastrous freezing temperatures that seriously checked farm activities. Minimum temperatures of 19 and 20 were recorded March 27 and 28. Some snow, driven by lashing winds, fell at this time. Foliage on trees and shrubs, early gardens and fruit bloom were killed. Alfalfa that was about 6 to 8 inches high on the upland was badly frozen back. About half the length of the leaves on spring oats was killed. Winter barley and winter oats and wheat were also severely set back, but recovery of small grains in most instances has been quite satisfactory. Some fields of volunteer oats that had jointed on bottom land were killed. In the wheat variety test, Nebraska No. 28 had jointed and will likely be a complete failure. Early Blackhull was also noticeably injured. All other varieties will likely make a complete recovery.

Lawton, continued:

Sweet clover seedings that have been in progress since December 15 and emerging to good stands were uninjured by the March freezes.

Fruits have been completely eliminated, with the exception of some apples, cherries, and grapes; the last shows some injury. Growth of foliage on trees and shrubs is being renewed very slowly.

March has been distinguished from the preceding months by several periods of high wind velocity and subnormal temperatures. A very light skift of snow fell March 30, but it melted as it fell. A heavy, killing frost was recorded March 29. The last heavy frost was recorded April 5 with a minimum temperature of 31 degrees. Frost on this date, however, did not seem to be injurious.

The monthly precipitation for the season is as follows: January, .82 inch; February, 1.84 inches; March, 1.76 inches. The excess for the three months amounts to .61 inch.

WOODWARD:

Precipitation totaling 4.00 inches fell between March 18 and 30. This was followed by a low temperature of 10 degrees which froze the tender new growth that rains had stimulated. This did not permanently injure wheat, which has since made a rank and rapid growth. It did more serious damage to arborvitaes and other half hard trees and shrubs than anyother low temperatures in the history of the station. Peaches were in full bloom, and, of course, blossoms were all killed. Buds of cherry trees were also killed to a large extent, and buds of grapes suffered to some extent. Many of the arborvitaes which have shown no winter injury in fifteen years were so badly injured some may die.

This week wound up the planting of half a million seedlings and cuttings of trees and grape vines to be grown for distribution to farmers on the shelterbelt and windbreak project.

The basement for the storage of material to be distributed was started. It is found impossible during our mild winters to keep material dormant unless it is stored in a basement or other structure where temperatures may be kept low. Some miscellaneous repair work on station buildings was also started.

19

NOTE:

> Attention of field men is invited to "Instructions on Plant
>
> Patents" covered by Memorandum 614, contained in Official
>
> Record of April 11, 1931, page 117.

- -

NOTE:

(C O P Y)

B.P.I. Memo. 566

March 4, 1931.

MEMORANDUM FOR HEADS OF OFFICES.

Gentlemen:

We are in receipt of a memorandum from the Secretary relative to delays in answering correspondence, reading in part as follows:

"Several complaints have reached the Department recently concerning delays in answering correspondence. While I can appreciate the fact that it is not always possible to make an immediate reply, I feel that all letters received in the Department are entitled to prompt attention and that in cases where a full reply cannot be made in a reasonable time, the receipt of the letter should at least be acknowledged and the writer advised that a more complete answer will be made at a later date."

It will be appreciated if you will bring this matter to the attention of all those in your organization who are engaged in handling correspondence with instructions that all letters received be acknowledged promptly if an immediate reply is not practicable.

Very sincerely,

sgd. Wm. A. Taylor

Chief of Bureau.

NOTE:

Under date of April 14, 1931, Director W. W. Stockberger issued
P. B. A. Circular No. 167, reading, as follows:

"Amending P.B.A. Circular No.161, 'Motor Fuels Tax Exemption
Procedure.'

"Circular letter No. 42, January 16, 1931, of the Chief
Coordinator, reads as follows:

Several instances have been brought to the attention
of this office where field activities of executive departments
and establishments are using Standard Forms Nos. 44 and 1066
(U. S. Government Motor Fuels Tax Exemption Certificate and
Receipt) in connection with the purchase of products, notably
lubricating oil, upon which no State or local tax is assessed.
It is deemed advisable to point out that in such instances
where there is no tax assessment upon the product purchased the use
of Standard Forms Nos. 44 and 1066 is clearly unnecessary and
unauthorized.
It is, therefore, suggested that heads of departments
and establishments issue instructions to their agents so as to
confine the use of these forms by their agents to the purpose for
which promulgated.

"Employees of the Department are requested to take note of
the foregoing instructions. It is well to bear in mind that the exemption form is intended primarily as evidence to be presented by the
exempting dealer to the State officers in support of his, the dealer's
claim for rebate of taxes previously paid by him. If it can not
serve this purpose, its use is obviously superfluous and unwarranted."

sgd.   W. W. Stockberger

Director.

WEEKLY STATION REPORTS

OF THE OFFICE OF

DRY LAND AGRICULTURE INVESTIGATIONS

BUREAU OF PLANT INDUSTRY

U. S. DEPARTMENT OF AGRICULTURE
APR 18 1931

REPORTS FOR THE WEEK ENDING APRIL 18, 1931.

HAVRE:

Temperatures during the past week have been about normal for
this season of the year. There was only a trace of precipitation. Wind
velocities have been unusually high even for this time of the year. The
average hourly velocity for the past seven days was approximately 10 miles
per hour. On three days, especially on the 17th, it was very high during
most of the day and a great many fields have blown rather badly. Only on
the 17th did any of the soil on the station blow.

Field work consisted in continuing of seed-bed preparation with
some early seeding of small grains. Most of the spring plowing for grains,
corn and flax is now completed. Work in the commercial fields is just
starting.

There was quite a lot of killing of domestic grasses at this
station during the winter. The greatest injury was to slender wheat grass.
In some of the plots in both broadcast and 3-foot rows, the injury was close
to 90 per cent. Some of this occurred in the recent plantings and some in
the older ones. Brome-grass was also injured, especially on the higher land,
but this injury seems to be mostly on the more recent plantings. The older
plants will apparently come out of it. Crested wheat grass shows practically
no killing. Contrasts are very noticeable between crested and slender wheat
grass.

Some additional plantings were made during the week in the
landscaping plan around the office building.
Maximum temperature 76; minimum 32; precipitation, trace.

JUDITH BASIN:

A rain of .54 inch the night of April 13 has improved surface
soil conditions. Since the rain the grass has greened up and has made some
growth. Crested wheat grass has produced sufficient growth to make good
pasture. Alfalfa and sweet clover are just beginning to show a few green
shoots. The moisture has minimized the soil blowing in this immediate
locality, although it was severe in some sections of the Judith Basin during
two days of the week. A light snow fell last night.

2

Judith Basin, continued:

A severe outbreak of Army cutworms is causing a great amount of damage to winter wheat fields in the Judith Basin. Fields seeded in stubble have suffered the greatest damage. However, some damage has been done to wheat seeded on fallow.

Field work during the week consisted of setting out 5,000 trees, one-half of which were conifers, cultivation of alfalfa, sweet clover and grass plots for the control of weeds.
Maximum temperature 74; minimum 27; precipitation, .57 inch.

HUNTLEY:

A shower on April 14 kept teams out of the field until the 16th. Seeding of all small grains was completed in the rotations before the rain and the moisture received, together with that already in the seedbeds, should insure prompt germination. The shower was of particular value to fall-sown grains, pastures, and alfalfa, which crops have made marked progress during the week. Weeds have also come into prominence in the last day or two on land which has not been cultivated this spring.

Dry-farmers throughout this region are plowing or cultivating land for fallow. Where injury to winter wheat has been more or less severe some reseeding to spring wheat is being done. The numerous inquiries which have reached the station concerning tillage methods and yields of barley, oats and flax indicates the possibility of using these crops to replace some of the acreage usually devoted to wheat production.
Maximum temperature 80; minimum 28; precipitation, .30 inch.

SHERIDAN:

Seeding of all early seedings of spring grain, field peas, alfalfa, grasses, and sweet clover was completed during the week. Fall plowing for corn and other late seeded crops was duckfooted, except in the rotation field.

The weather continued warm and dry. Wheat, oats, and barley, sown the first half of the week of April 11, emerged. Grass is making a fair growth, but alfalfa and sweet clover have been slow in starting. Winter wheat made a good growth during the week.

3

Sheridan, continued:

      All of the roofs of the station buildings, except the Superintendent's residence and the ice house, were sprayed. A trace of moisture, which would have prevented the shingles from absorbing the spray properly, stopped work on those buildings to-day, April 18.
    Maximum temperature 80; minimum 29; precipitation, trace.

DICKINSON:

      Warm, dry weather continued through the week with wind enough on three days to cause some soil blowing. The surface of the soil is becoming so dry that grain seeded now is likely to have uneven stands unless rain comes soon.

      Oats were seeded on the Rotations on April 13 and barley was seeded on the 14th. Wheat, oats and barley varieties were seeded April 16 and 17.

      Winter wheat and rye came through the winter with better stands than for several years. Where winter wheat was seeded on fallow on Rotation 569 a good stand survived for the first time during the six years of the test. Winter wheat seeded in grain stubble, on corn stubble, and in standing corn stalks, has good stands and about the same amount of growth on all three methods.

      Grasses have greened up rapidly during the week but need rain for further growth. Crested wheatgrass now shows more growth than either slender wheatgrass or brome-grass. A good many inquiries are still being received for crested wheatgrass seed. Orders for all of the station seed were received about two months ago.

      Precipitation to date in April amounts to .18 inch.
    Maximum temperature 82; minimum 29; precipitation, none.

4

MANDAN:

Agronomy

The past week has been favorable for all field work. The wind was above average in velocity throughout the week.

The preparation of all plots was finished early in the week. Wheat was seeded on the 15th, oats on the 16th, barley, peas, sweet clover, and brome-grass on the 17th. The average date of wheat seeding is the 18th and oats the 21st.

While the soil is now dry on the surface, moisture conditions are favorable for starting all small grains.

Crested wheatgrass and brome-grass made a good growth during the week, and alfalfa made a good start. Native vegetation is making good progress, and the prairie is green in some spots.
Maximum temperature 83; minimum 33; precipitation, none.

Arboriculture

As large a crew as possible has been engaged during the week planting stock in the station nurseries, and packing trees to farmer cooperators. Good headway has been made with the shipping, and it is hoped the hardwood tree shipments will be completed in good time next week.

Very much needed repairs to the east wall of the greenhouse have been completed, and a crew is now engaged in making repairs to the concrete sidewalks around the station buildings.

Horticulture

Pruning, painting pruning wounds, and hauling brush have occupied most of the week. Grapes in the field and buds in the nursery have been uncovered. Some new strawberry selections furnished by the Horticultural Office were planted on April 17. Golden currant selections are being planted in the South field. Nursery planting is being held up in the hope that rain will put the ground in better condition for this small stuff.

5

BELLE FOURCHE:

Warm, windy weather has prevailed throughout most of the week. No precipitation occurred, and the strong winds have caused the surface soil to dry so rapidly that much of the grain seeded last week on corn ground and plowed land will not germinated until after rain is received. Practically no germination has taken place on spring plowed land, but apparently most of the grain on fallow has germinated and should emerge within a few days.

Winter wheat has made distinct improvement and is now in excellent condition. Winter rye, alfalfa, and brome-grass have also made a good growth. Lack of moisture, however, threatens the further development of all crops. Brome-grass has exhaust d nearly all of the available moisture in the soil, and only a small reserve of moisture remains in the soil o winter rye and older alfalfa plots.
Maximum temperature 84; minimum 31; precipitation, none.

ARCHER:

The weather has been dry and favorable for field work. However, the soil is becoming dry, making tillage more difficult.

The work at the station has consisted of breaking the ridges of 64 acres of fall listed land and duckfooting 34 acres to be seeded to corn and sunflowers. All tillage for wheat, oats, and barley on the rotation plots has been completed, plots staked, and the greater part of the spring wheat plots in these experiments have been seeded. The dates of seeding wheat, oats, barley, flax, safflower, and alfalfa were made April 15. The methods and dates of seeding corn were also made April 15. To-day, April 18, the trees are receiving further tillage and the land which is to be fallowed for spring grains in 1932 is being tilled with middle busters.

Winter wheat is doing well and the early grasses have made considerable growth. Some of the buds on the trees are about ready to burst.

Mr. J. R. Dawson, of the Bureau of Dairy Industry, visited the station April 15.
Maximum temperature 72; minimum 31; precipitation, none.

6

AKRON:

The past week was fair and unusually warm. General impression gained from vegetative growth indicates that spring is here, fully two weeks early. Native sod is greening and weeds, even including the pig weed, are emerging by myriads.

Cereal grain seeded late in March before the blizzard is well emerged. Cereal grain seeded early in April after the blizzard is emerging by this week-end.

The work of the past week consisted largely of work incident to the Third Annual Feeders' Day which was held Thursday, April 16. Also of work incident to the starting of the summer grazing experiment with fattening pigs. These pigs will be given the third of their initial weights to-morrow, Sunday, April 19.

A very interested crowd of some 300 individuals attended the Feeders' Day meeting on Thursday, April 16. A very good delegation from the Denver Stock Yards was present this year for the first time. Space will not permit the listing of the distinguished visitors present.

Iris is in bloom this week-end.
Maximum temperature 80; minimum 34; precipitation, trace.

NORTH PLATTE:

The weather has been dry and open, with moderate temperatures, medium to strong winds and no precipitation. Spring seeded grains have emerged, and winter wheat is making rapid growth.

The chief station activity of the week was preparation for and conducting of the Third Annual Judging Contest for Smith-Hughes high school teams on the 16th and 17th. There were 18 schools represented with 245 contestants. Contests were run in judging poultry, dairy and beef cattle, horses, hogs, sheep, wood working, dairy products, Babcock testing, grain judging and identification, grain grading, and public speaking.

COLBY:

The weather has been rather windy and unsettled this week. Light showers fell on the 15th. The warm winds melted what was left of the snow and dried out the surface soil considerably.

All crops are making excellent growth. The spring small grains came up to good stands the first of the week. Weeds are also starting.

The field adjoining the present rotation project on the south was laid out for the new rotations. The plots will be staked out the first of the week, preparatory to cutting out the roadways and alleys and starting the tillage on the plots to be fallowed this year.

Getting rid of volunteer wheat on plots in the project that were in wheat last year promises to be a problem this year. On most of these plots there is a fairly thick and very vigorous growth of volunteer wheat.

The combine, mounted on our Caterpillar tractor in the shop at the Hays Experiment Station, has arrived. A very neat job of mounting was done, and the outfit looks as though it ought to do the work in excellent manner.

Maximum temperature 82; minimum 33; precipitation, .13 inch.

GARDEN CITY:

Spring plowing was finished on Monday, April 13. A sub-surface packer was used following the plowing. It seems to have helped a great deal in holding the moisture in the furrow slice.

Soil samples were taken on the M. C. Winter Wheat series April 16. On the A and B plots the upper three feet seem well supplied with moisture. Below that area the ground is quite deficient in available moisture. Wheat is making abnormal heavy growth for this time of the year. Much of the wheat is 10 to 12 inches high.

The fore part of the week was very windy. Temperatures were up in the 70's every day. All vegetation is making rapid growth. Weeds are coming fast.

Maximum temperature 78; minimum 35; precipitation, .03 inch.

8

HAYS:

Winter wheat continues to make heavy growth and has already commenced lodging on fallowed plots. Winter rye, unlike the winter wheat, has not made such heavy growth except on the edges of the plots. As a matter of fact the rye looks bad. It is about ready to head. All spring planted grains are looking fine except for the weeds coming in the plots.

Only about three and one-half days during the week were suitable for tillage work, there having been enough rain together with the cloudy, damp weather to keep the soil wet. During the time when tillage work could be done strenuous efforts were made to destroy the oats (sown for cover crop last fall in the roads), winter wheat and weeds in the roads and alleys. During the week sign boards and labeled stakes have been placed at points of most interest over the project.
Maximum temperature 77; minimum 37; precipitation, .40 inch.

TUCUMCARI:

The past week has been comparatively cloudy, but with only .10 inch precipitation. Field work has consisted primarily of listing and field cultivating. Yucca was grubbed from sod strips between tree rows and considerable pruning of orchard trees performed. Last year many fruit trees were so seriously injured by severe drought that a great amount of wood died, but the extent of injury was difficult to determine until leaves emerged.

Conditions remain favorable for wheat and for early field work.
Maximum temperature 80; minimum 42; evaporation, 1.699 inches.
Wind velocity, 7.2 miles per hour.

DALHART:

Two showers totalling .58 inch have hastened materially the spring growth of all vegetation. Field work and the completion of planting trees and shrubs has been delayed for the past three days. The showers were of unestimated value to plants already in the ground.

Winter wheat, winter rye, oats and barley are growing rapidly. Winter rye is jointing now. Winter wheat covers the ground with a very dense growth for this time of the year. Oats and barley did not appear to be very good before the rains.

9

Dalhart, continued:

The last date of sweet clover seeding was made on the 15th. Soil moisture sample s from the winter wheat plots still shows ample moisture for normal growth.

Maximum temperature 80; minimum 37; precipitation, .58 inch. Wind velocity, 8.8 miles per hour; evaporation, 1.539 inches.

BIG SPRING:

Cloudy weather has prevailed during the past week with rain threatening on most every day. Three very light rains were received during this time. Trees and shrubs are starting to recover from the set back they received from the last freeze. Little green leaves are starting to show amid the brown color.

Field work during the week has consisted of hoeing weeds from the tree rows and in cleaning up the grounds. Considerable time is required for grinding and mixing feed used in the cattle feeding tests which are being conducted here. Three lots of ten head each are being fed for a period of 140 days. The following rations are being used:

Lot 1 - ground milo heads, cottonseed meal, chopped Sumac fodder.
Lot 2 - ground milo heads, cottonseed meal, chopped Sumac fodder, alfalfa hay.
Lot 3 - ground milo heads, cottonseed meal, cottonseed hulls, alfalfa hay.

The feeding period will close on May 8 at which time a Feeders' Day meeting will be held here.

Maximum temperature 83; minimum 47; precipitation, .19 inch.

LAWTON:

The past week has been one of good growing weather, and field work has progressed steadily. Spring plowing of rotation plots, both cropped and fallow was completed, and a good many fall plowed and fallow plots were disked or knifed. March freezes were not injurious to weeds and the spring growth has been hardy and persistent.

The M. C. corn plots were replanted April 14. Seeding of alfalfa and sweet clover rotation plots was done April 6, but stands are still unsatisfactory. The first cotton date planting was done April 15 on excellent seed-beds. The first planting of the chinch bug sorghum resistance project was made April 13.

10

Lawton, continued:

Small grain crops are growing rapidly and vigorously, and the plants present a rich, dark green, healthy color. Most of the wheat is knee high or better, and several plots of barley are heading as well as some of the September seeded winter oats. Considerable border injury from freezing weather in March exists on the winter oats and winter barley plots. This injury is accounted for by the fact that a good deal of jointing occurred before the freeze. Nebraska No. 28 now looks as though it would make a 25 or 30 per cent recovery.

Several threats of rain during the week finally resulted in .45 inch. The maximum temperature for the week was 80.

WOODWARD:

The weather the first part of the week was dry and windy, but the last half of the week has been cloudy with a few small showers occurring. Wheat has made a rapid growth and trees and shrubs that were not injured by the late freezes are beginning to make a good showing of leaf.

Station work for the week consisted of planting a variety of nursery stock and cuttings, and work on the basement of the new laboratory building has been pushed as rapidly as possible.

Station visitors for the week were Dr. H. G. Bennett, Mr. D. P. Trent, and other officials of the Oklahoma A. & M. College.

ARDMORE:

The weather during the week was mild with moderate wind velocity and no precipitation.

Cultivated pasture plants and all early native vegetation made a noticeable growth. Some species of weeds such as little bind weeds, Russian thistle and tansy mustard became noticeable early in the week.

Barley, oats and wheat seeded on the larger fields emerged on the 14th. Barley and wheat on the main rotation plots emerged on the 18th.

Variety tests plots for barley, flax, oats, and wheat, and flax plots in the main rotations were seeded during the week.
Maximum temperature 80; minimum 27; precipitation, none.

6

WEEKLY STATION REPORTS

OF THE OFFICE OF

DRY LAND AGRICULTURE INVESTIGATIONS

BUREAU OF PLANT INDUSTRY

U. S. DEPARTMENT OF AGRICULTURE

REPORTS FOR THE WEEK ENDING APRIL 25, 1931.

HAVRE:

        Weather conditions during the past week have continued to be
unfavorable. Wind velocity on April 19 was extremely high. Minimum
temperatures were below freezing every night during the week, reaching
a minimum of 17 degrees on one night. There has been considerable damage
from wind in certain localities. We have had very little soil blowing,
however, on the station. What damage there was has been limited to small
areas in corn stubble that had not been cultivated this spring.

        Surface soil at this station this spring is a little different
from what it usually is. Ordinarily there is a great deal of crusting
while this spring the surface is much more flocculent.

        With all the adverse conditions, winter wheat looks as thrifty
as it has since the station was started. Stands generally are 100 per cent.

        Some of the early seedings of spring rye, wheat, and barley are
up. Preparation of seed beds for small grains on the rotations is completed
and seeding has started. Drilling is being done on the commercial fields
also.

        Range conditions over this section are not very favorable at
this time. Water supply in many of the mountain streams is low and grass
is starting rather slowly.

        Professor F. M. Harrington, of the Montana Experiment Station,
visited the station on April 25, in regard to the shelter belt and landscaping work.
        Maximum temperature 57; minimum 17; precipitation, .02 inch.

JUDITH BASIN:

        The strong winds of April 17 to 19 were followed by a light
snow-fall April 20 and a heavy snow-storm on April 21. Since then the
weather has been cool with a minimum of 10 degrees being record the night
of April 22. The snow has practically all melted, but fields are still
very muddy in spots where snow drifted. The high winds, cutworms and low
temperatures have caused further deterioration of winter wheat.
        Maximum temperature 49; minimum 10; precipitation, .14 inch.

2

HUNTLEY:

A light snow-storm early in the week has been followed by cold weather and one or two windy days. Spring-sown grains are sprouting but their progress has been somewhat retarded by cold, and in some places the seed beds have dried out to the extent that moisture will be needed to bring up the seedlings. Fall-sown grains are growing slowly but alfalfa and cultivated grasses have developed rapidly during the week.

The seeding of grain varieties has been completed and plowing for corn has begun. Miscellaneous fallow plots were plowed with the duck-foot cultivator to check the growth of weeds and volunteer grain, which came up in the stubble after the rain of a week ago. The duckfoot has replaced the moldboard plow in preparing this series of plots for fallow during the last three years.

Maximum temperature 59; minimum 13; precipitation, trace.

SHERIDAN:

Cold, cloudy weather with high winds prevailed over the first part of the week. Temperatures moderated somewhat over the last part of the week, but freezing has occurred each night. Light snow fell at the station on April 22, and much heavier snow south and west, as much as 17 inches being recorded within about 15 miles of the station.

Some fencing was done the first part of the week. Planting of the shelter belt spacing experiment was started the 23rd and is being completed to-day, April 25. Seedings in the date-of-seeding experiments with wheat, oats, barley, and flax were made on the 24th. Land that has been cultivated this spring is getting quite dry on the surface, but moisture still remains close to the surface on land not yet touched this spring. Growth of all vegetation was slow during the week. Field peas seeded early last week are just beginning to emerge. Spring wheat sown the 11th also is emerging.

It appears now that the loss of Northwest poplar from killing over the winter in the shelter belt was heavy. Nearly half of those in the block adjoining the highway, and a much larger proportion of those in the west row of the 12x12 block immediately south of the railroad, are dead. There appears to be no killing in the east row of the latter block.

3

Sheridan, continued:

      Spraying of the roofs of the station buildings is being completed to-day, April 25. Because of the damp weather no work on the roofs was possible this week until to-day.
    Maximum temperature 50; minimum 15; precipitation, .11 inch.
    Precipitation, Sheridan Weather Bureau Station, .49 inch.

DICKINSON:

      The weather of the week was cold, dry and windy. Minimum temperatures were below freezing each night and were below 20 degrees on five nights. The freezing each night combined with the dry soil has set back the vegetation to some extent.

      Some miscellaneous planting of increase grains was done during the week. All of the fallow and corn ground to be planted later was cultivated with the duckfoot to stop blowing. About 40 rods of woven wire fence along the east line were pulled out with the tractor. Soil had blown from the corn field to the west and covered the wire completely in places.

      Hardy varieties of vegetables and potatoes were planted in the garden on April 23 and 24. The garden soil is so dry that some of the seed will not grow until rain comes.

      Poisoned-bran was spread over most of the alfalfa to try to stop the cutworms, which have shown up in considerable numbers and at present are working mainly in alfalfa. These seem to be an army-cutworm and if dry weather continues may cause more trouble after the grain emerges.

      Crested wheatgrass in rows was cultivated to kill the volunteer plants which came in from seed shattered at harvest.

      Visitors included Director P. F. Trowbridge and Mr. W. J. Church of the Board of Administration.
    Maximum temperature 55; minimum 13; precipitation, .02 inch.

4

MANDAN:

Agronomy

The past week has been cool with freezing temperatures every night. Rain fell on the 19th with a trace of snow.

Most of the week was spent in cultivating and plowing seed and feed blocks. All perennial row crops were cultivated.

Some work has been done on the roadways in spots where washing had taken place. The spots were filled and seeded down.

Peppergrass is thick all over the station again this year. The good fall rains gave it an excellent start last fall.

Crested wheatgrass is now 6 or 8 inches high and would have made good pasture a week or 10 days ago.

Small grain seeded 10 days ago is not up. It has been retarded by the cool weather.
Maximum temperature 57; minimum 20; precipitation, .22 inch.

Arboriculture

Shipment of shelter-belt trees has been continued during the week. Trees for planting new 1931 shelter belts have been shipped to 84 farmers in Montana, 94 farmers in North Dakota, 71 farmers in South Dakota, and 40 farmers in Wyoming. Trees for replacing losses in 1930 plantings have been shipped to 231 farmers in the four states.

Evergreens are now being dug preparatory to shipping the early part of next week.

Land has been prepared for the planting of 70,000 Northwest poplar cuttings.

Horticulture

The cold weather of the past week was beneficial in that it held back growth and discouraged too early blooming.

Work during the week included planting the nursery and replacements in the field, blight work, hauling brush so as to clear the fields for cultivating, and shipping fruit trees to horticultural cooperators.

5

Mandan, continued:

Horticulture, continued.

The planting of vegetable seed for the various projects under way at the station was started March 15. A fine assortment of plants has been raised and transplanted to cold frames.

A new shrubbery border, enclosing the back yards of the Super-intendent and Assistant Agronomist, was started this spring. The shrubbery groups on this ground are being renovated, older and dead specimens removed, and new bushes planted. There is little winter killing apparent so far compared to last spring. The last week's frosty weather has endangered the blossom buds of lilacs, which are unusually abundant this year. It is still a little early to determine if any damage has been done.

The first seeding in the acre and coulee gardens was started April 10. This is the earliest date of outdoor seeding of vegetables on record at the station. Peas, radishes and spinach are up so far.

A new bed of asparagus was planted April 24. The variety Mary Washington was selected for the work. Two-year plants raised at the station were used. Two planting systems are employed, 6 feet by 1½ feet, and 4 feet by 2½ feet.

BELLE FOURCHE:

The weather has been cloudy, threatening, and abnormally cold. Killing frosts occurred every night, and unusually low temperatures did considerable damage to crops, trees, and shrubbery. High winds prevailed during the fore part of the week, and sufficient soil blowing took place to injure small grain slightly. Aside from a trace of snow on April 20, no precipitation has been received since April 1 and 2 when the negligible total of .13 inch precipitation was recorded; and the month to date is next to the driest April on record.

The lack of moisture has become quite serious with reference to both the germination of crops and the supply of water for livestock on the range. The surface 3 to 4 inches of soil is perfectly dry and no moisture is present below a depth of seven inches, except after green manure crops and summer fallow. Crop prospects, as a whole, are the most unfavorable they have been for years.

6

Belle Fourche, continued:

     Owing to the cold weather, no perceptible growth has been made
by fall grain, hay, or pasture crops. Spring grain is coming up slowly
and unevenly, but better stands apparently will be obtained on most of
the plots than previously anticipated. A considerable portion of the
seed, however, has not germinated and good stands will not be obtained
until after rain is received. A small amount of grain emerged early in
the week, but was frozen back to the ground. The tips of winter rye
and winter wheat were killed by the frost and some damage was done to
alfalfa. The severe frosts the past week have apparently killed most of
the fruit buds which escaped the sub-zero weather the latter part of
March. Likewise extensive injury was done to lilacs, spirea, and other
shrubs.
     Maximum temperature 57; minimum 14; precipitation, trace.

ARDMORE:

     The weather during the week was cold and blustering. There were
three periods of precipitation with the total insufficient to add any
amount to soil moisture content.

     Temperatures were unusually low and caused considerable damage
to early garden crops, ornamental shrubs, fruit trees and alfalfa. Barley
and oats were badly frozen but no heavy permanent damage was noticed.
Cultivated pasture plants, spring wheat and some winter wheat plots were
damaged to a limited extent.

     Spring plowing of plots for beans, corn and sorgo was completed
during the week.

     The stocker steers on winter feeding experiment were weighed on
the 24th. The following table gives the pounds gain per head made during
the course of the experiment to date:

Period	1	2	3	4	5	Total gain
Alfalfa and Straw	8.9	4.6	10.4	-2.3	9.6	31.2
Silage and Straw	8.8	6.9	-25.8	13.1	8.1	-6.5
Sorgo	1.9	5.8	3.1	2.3	22.7	35.8

    Maximum temperature 47; minimum 18; precipitation, .09 inch, with
1½ inches of snow.

ARCHER:

During the first half of the week the weather was cold and
threatening and during the last half stormy. Considerable wind prevailed
during the fore part of the week, making field work almost impossible.
Snow began to fall April 22 and continued until the morning of April 24.
There was but very little wind during the storm and the snow melted where
it fell. The total precipitation was .33 inch.

Work at the station has consisted of digging holes for the
transplanting of trees and the digging of wild plum sprouts which were
out of bounds. Some gravel was hauled on the roadway. Since the storm
the seed potatoes have been sorted and dipped. The reconstruction of the
fence west of the farmstead is under way.

The frost recorded the morning of April 21 froze all spring
crops that were up except Safflower. The early seeding of flax is ruined.
It is expected that the spring wheat, oats, and barley that were up will
survive.
    Maximum temperature 65; minimum 11; precipitation, .33 inch.

AKRON:

The fore part of the week was open and favorable for field work.
The later part of the week has been dominated by cloudy weather with
intermittent snow storms. It was snowing this morning, April 25, at the
time readings were taken so that yesterday's precipitation was not taken.
This snow has continued to the present time, about 11:00 a.m., and it now
looks like the ground was covered with seven to eight inches of snow.
This snow is composed of large heavy flakes and is falling evenly over the
surface of the ground. There is a slight drift of air from the north.

Second date of seeding spring grains was made on the 20th. First
date of seeding corn was made on the 20th. Rotation stubble plots for corn
and for fallow were partially disked before the team was driven from the
field by a heavy damp snow-storm. Volunteer winter wheat is very dense on
some of these plots. Other field work consisted of seeding the artichokes
and small grains for hay in the general forage variety experiment. Other
outside work consisted of some finishing touches to the summer-pasturing
pig lots across the railroad.

Rotation small grain plots were practically emerged before the
storms of this week-end.

8

Akron, continued:

Trees were received this week-end for the cooperative snow fence planting along the railroad right-of-way, just south of the station building plot. This planting is to be composed of Chinese Elm and Rocky Mountain Red Cedar (Juniper).
Maximum temperature 72; minimum 19; precipitation, .22 inch.

NORTH PLATTE:

Temperatures for the week have been subnormal, with a considerable amount of cloudiness and precipitation in the form of snow. Minimum temperatures of 24 and 21 were recorded on April 21 and 25, respectively. The latter was the low for the month. Snow fell almost continuously from the morning of April 23 until the evening of the next day. Total precipitation was .75 inch.

Experimental potatoes were planted early in the week. No other field work was accomplished.

COLBY:

After having an almost delightful spring all winter we are having a rather disagreeable winter almost all spring. The weather this week has been windy, cold, and snowy. Over night Monday, April 20, the temperature dropped to 21, freezing the surface of the ground, and killing whatever fruit buds escaped the March blizzard. All the rank wheat, such as on the fallow plots, which was from 12 inches to 16 inches high, was laid flat as though rolled with a heavy roller. Before it had a chance to come up again it began snowing, covering it. The snow has continued during the last three days, but not much more than four inches fell all told. Much of it melted as it fell, although the temperature has remained below freezing during most of the time. Farmers are much concerned about the wheat. Although almost flat on the ground it has a good color and does not appear to be hurt otherwise. The spring grains show no effects whatever.

The plots were lined up preparatory to trimming the first of the week, but no trimming has been possible since. The tillage of the roadways and alleys will be done as soon as the ground is workable.
Maximum temperature 69; minimum 21; precipitation, .63 inch.
Snow, April 20, 2.00 inches; April 23, 24 and 25, 4.50 inches.

9

GARDEN CITY:

The past week has been cloudy, cold and wet most of the time. Field work has been at a standstill on account of frequent rains. Some alleys were cultivated out with a five-tooth on April 22. Minimum temperatures have been near freezing or slightly below all week.

If weather conditions permit, the spring plowing of fallows will be done next week. Weed growth is starting rapidly and from now on a great deal of cultivation will be required to keep plots clean.

Roadways were drilled to wheat last September to prevent soil blowing and washing. At present the wheat is nearly a foot and one-half high. It will be cut for hay the latter part of May and the roadways kept clean cultivated the remainder of the summer. This method has been very effective in preventing erosion.

Maximum temperature 75; minimum 27; precipitation, 1.01 inches.

TUCUMCARI:

The week has been characterized by long periods of cloudiness, followed by high winds. Considerable increase land was field cultivated or listed, for weed growth and wind movement necessitated early cultivation. The spring plowed plots in the rotations and M.C. series are being plowed. This is somewhat earlier than usual for spring plowing on the station, but early weed growth and abundant moisture combine to make this appear advisable.

Tree rows, vineyard, and orchard have been spring-tooth-harrowed. Early growth of the recently planted trees has in most cases been very encouraging.

Some seventy native cedars and pinon pines were secured at the cap-rock by the station force this week and planted on the station.

Maximum temperature 84; minimum 32; precipitation, .18 inch.

Wind velocity, 7.7 miles per hour; evaporation, 1.446 inches.

DALHART:

   The weather the past week has ranged from days or parts of days which were characterized by high winds and high amount of soil in the air to rainy, misty, foggy weather. It was almost impossible to get field work or other outside work done with any satisfaction. A heavy freeze with a high wind occurred on the night of April 20. Some vegetation was severely nipped while other vegetation was barely touched. The latter part of the week, with the exception of this afternoon which is windy and cold, has been misty and foggy most of the time.

   Winter wheat, rye, sweet clover, and native grass are growing fast. Most of the trees and shrubs are leafing out. Rye in a few instances is heading out. It is very spotted on all plots. Wheat, where there is ample moisture in the subsoil, is growing fast. Where the subsoil moisture is deficient the wheat shows a lack of vigor. Oats and barley are still rather yellowish from the setback experienced the last of March. Both of these crops are very small, barely out of the drill mark.

   Some plowing was done during the week. Very little headway was made with this operation because of the extremely unfavorable weather. The blueweed plots, where the treatment is given, were plowed during the week. Progress is evident towards eradication of blueweed by some of the methods being used.

   Cherries are just now blooming. It is too early in the season to forecast the set of fruit. The grape vines are swelling buds.

   The second-year sweet clover seedings are making wonderful growth. The late seedings for this year, at the present time, are showing thick stands while the earlier seedings were thinned by unfavorable and unseasonable weather conditions.
 Maximum temperature 80; minimum 28; precipitation, .14 inch.
 Wind velocity, 9.8 miles per hour; evaporation, 1.109 inches.

BIG SPRING:

   Although the temperature did not get down to the freezing point; an unusually late norther visited this section April 20. It was a gentle reminder that soil and air temperatures were too cold for planting purposes. Rain occurred on two days during the week, but the total only amounted to .25 inch.

11

Big Spring, continued:

Station work has consisted mainly of cultivating fallows, leveling listed plots, and sand furrowing. Considerable time was also spent in grubbing the pasture preparatory to getting the land ready for future tree planting.

Mr. Sterling Evans, District Agent of the Texas Extension Service, was a station visitor during the week.
Maximum temperature 88; minimum 41; precipitation, .25 inch.

LAWTON:

A week of cold, showery weather has been favorable to the continued rapid growth and development of small grains. Winter barley is practically in full head and heading of winter oats has made some progress.

Practically all of the sorghums seeded April 13 in the chinch bug resistance project are emerging to good stands. Several varieties show strong, vigorous germination while others are slower, emerging rather unevenly.

Cotton varieties planted April 15 are only sprouted, and corn that was replanted on the rotation plots April 14 is sprouted and emerging very slowly.

The minimum temperature dropped to 30 on the night of April 21 and a heavy, killing frost was recorded on the morning of the 22nd. Beans were killed, potato tops were killed back to the surface, and growing corn was nipped back to the extent of one-half of its growth. Sweet clover and alfalfa, much of it in the 2 and 3-leaf stage, seem to have been uninjured. Some additional injury is evident on the grapes.

Seven showers from April 16 to 24, inclusive, netted a total of .93 inch.
Maximum temperature 58; minimum 30.

12

WOODWARD:

The past week has been cool with fog and slow drizzling rains.
Time has been devoted to repair work on buildings, running concrete on
root cellar, hoeing weeds and planting the last few evergreen seedlings.
A trip was made to the canyons where about three thousand red cedar
seedlings were collected.

Due to the abundance of rain in March and the almost continuous
cloudy weather and light showers in April winter wheat is making a very
rapid growth.

Because of the damaging freeze the last of March and the cool
weather since, trees and shrubbery are only now coming into leaf again.
Gardening operations which were very active a month ago have since been
almost at a standstill.

Chinese arborvitae trees, which have shown no sign of winter
injury in fifteen years, were in many cases injured so severely about
Woodward by the March freeze that some of them will no doubt die and most
of them will be crippled. It is understood that great injury was suffered
by evergreen material usually hardy, as far south as Fort Worth. This was
due probably to the fact that warm weather and abundant rainfall had started
it into rapid new growth and the severe freeze was too much for it in that
condition. The bark on some trees was actually burst, as a water pipe is.
In Kansas the same material that was killed further south was not injured
because it was still dormant.

- - - - - - -

NOTE:

Under date of April 22, 1931, Doctor Wm. A. Taylor, Chief of
Bureau, issued B. P. I. Memo. 576, reading as follows:

"In the interest of simplification, the Office of the
Secretary has suggested the standard use of the term "Division"
to designate units reporting directly to the Chief of Bureau. It
is believed that the use of this term generally will be helpful
to people outside of the Department in understanding references
to branches of the Bureau, whether appearing in publications or
in correspondence. Accordingly, hereafter all branches of the
Bureau heretofore referred to as offices or laboratories will be
known as Divisions. This terminology to be uniform should be used
in connection with letterheads, correspondence generally and in all
printed matter where the title of the unit is used."